shining

CAROLINA M. VEIRA

BOOK SERIES BY FIG FACTOR MEDIA

WordPower Book Series

© Copyright 2021, Fig Factor Media, LLC.
All rights reserved.

All rights reserved. No portion of this book may be reproduced by mechanical, photographic or electronic process, nor may it be stored in a retrieval system, transmitted in any form or otherwise be copied for public use or private use without written permission of the copyright owner.

It is sold with the understanding that the publisher and the individual authors are not engaged in the rendering of psychological, legal, accounting or other professional advice. The content and views in each chapter are the sole expression and opinion of its author and not necessarily the views of Fig Factor Media, LLC.

For more information, contact:

Fig Factor Media, LLC | www.figfactormedia.com

Cover Design & Layout by Juan Pablo Ruiz
Printed in the United States of America

ISBN: 978-1-957058-00-9
Library of Congress Control Number: 2021923560

DEDICATION

To my family.
Because of you, I am, I dream, I do.

Los amo infinitamente,
-Caro

ACKNOWLEDGMENTS

Special thanks to Jackie Camacho-Ruiz. You are an incredible and unstoppable source of light, love, passion for life. I am lucky, blessed, honored to know you and call you, my friend. Thank you for your heart!

INTRO

"Shine so bright, that your shine will cover everything and everyone around you!

Our personal journeys are filled with opportunity. Opportunity to learn and grow, to understand others and to see things through a different lens. Our shine has unlimited impact, and everyone will benefit from it."

Shining:
To give out or reflect bright light. To be brilliant or excellent at something.

KEEP SHINING!
HOW BEAUTIFUL IT IS TO HELP OTHERS SHINE. WE ARE MOST EFFECTIVE IN DOING SO WHEN WE SHARE OUR STORIES AND EXPERIENCES WITH OTHERS. SOME CALL THIS MENTORING. OTHERS CALL IT COACHING. AT THE END OF THE DAY, IT IS ABOUT SHARING OUR VOICE TO EMPOWER OTHERS. WE NEED TO SHINE BRIGHT SO WE CAN COVER OTHERS WITH THAT BEAUTIFUL LIGHT.

KEEP WALKING! KEEP CREATING! KEEP SHINING!

"Only in darkness can you see the stars"

-MARTIN LUTHER KING, JR.

Am I being true to my personal beliefs, my values, and my why?

I WORK DAILY ON BEING ALIGNED TO MY BELIEFS AND MY VALUES; FROM WHAT I EAT TO THE JEWELRY I BUY. ALL THESE SMALL ACTIONS ARE LINKED TO MY PERSONAL BELIEFS, MY VALUES AND MY WHY.

Sparkle:
To be vivacious and witty.

I SPARKLE. YOU SPARKLE. WE SPARKLE

MAY YOUR GOALS BE SO BIG THAT THOSE AROUND YOU CALL YOU LUCKY, EXTRA, INTENSE, OR CRAZY. I, PERSONALLY, HAVE BEEN CALLED ALL THOSE THINGS AT SOME POINT IN MY LIFETIME. AND THIS CRITICISM ACTUALLY TRANSLATES INTO "YOU ARE DOING SOMETHING GREAT, KEEP AT IT!" ACCORDING TO THE CAMBRIDGE ENGLISH DICTIONARY, LUCK IS "THE FORCE THAT CAUSES THINGS, ESPECIALLY GOOD THINGS, TO HAPPEN TO YOU BY CHANCE AND NOT AS A RESULT OF YOUR OWN EFFORTS OR ABILITIES." THUS, IT IS NORMAL FOR OTHERS TO SEE THAT WHEN SOMETHING GREAT IS HAPPENING TO US, IT IS JUST PURE LUCK. BUT WE ALL KNOW THAT SHINING, LUCKY MOMENT WAS THE RESULT OF GRIT, TALENT, COMMITMENT, HARD WORK, AND BELIEVING IN YOURSELF.

I WISH YOU MANY MORE SPARKLING MOMENTS OF "LUCK" BECAUSE IT MEANS YOU ARE ON THE RIGHT TRACK. CHEERS!

"Nothing can dim the light that shines from within"

-MAYA ANGELOU

Are you influencing the world or constantly being influenced by the world?

ARE WE IN CONTROL OF OUR ACTIONS AND EMOTIONS, OR ARE WE ALLOWING THE CIRCUMSTANCES AROUND US MANAGE OUR LIVES? ARE WE BEING INTENTIONAL ABOUT HOW WE WANT TO LIVE OUR LIVES? WHAT DO WE NEED TO CHANGE TO SHINE MORE BRIGHTLY?

Glitter:
To shine due to strong feeling or inner sparkle.

HUMANS LIKE GLITTER.

WE ARE ATTRACTED TO ALL THINGS SHINY. OUR LOVE FOR GLITTER MIGHT BE ROOTED IN A PRIMITIVE DESIRE FOR WATER. IT ALSO SEEMS LINKED TO OUR LOVE FOR PRETTY THINGS. THESE ARE INTERESTING EXTREMES: ONE EXPLANATION IS TIED TO SURVIVAL AND THE NEXT ONE IS TIED TO FEELINGS. WHATEVER MEANING YOU GIVE TO GLITTER, WE CAN AGREE THAT GLITTER INVITES US ALL TO HAVE MOMENTS OF HAPPINESS. IT MAKES US SMILE, EVEN IF FOR A FEW NANOSECONDS. IT HELPS US DREAM OF BRIGHTER DAYS.

"The place where light and dark begin to touch is where miracles arise"

- ROBERT A. JOHNSON

What advice would you give to your 13-year-old self?

I LOVE TO ASK THIS QUESTION FOR TWO REASONS.

REASON 1: IT TYPICALLY REMINDS US OF SOMETHING WE ALREADY KNOW BUT TEND TO FORGET ABOUT OUR REASONS TO GO FOR SOMETHING.

REASON 2: YOUNGER GENERATIONS CAN BENEFIT FROM OUR WORDS OF INSPIRATION, OUR CHALLENGES, AND THE WAY WE PIVOT AND ACHIEVE SUCCESS.

Glow:
To feel deep pleasure or satisfaction and convey it through expression and bearing.

"If you want to give light to others you have to glow yourself".
-THOMAS S. MONSON

I KEEP COMING BACK TO THIS IDEA: WE NEED TO LOVE OUR SHINE, OUR GLOW, OUR SPARKLE. WE NEED TO LEARN TO ACCEPT SINCERE WORDS. JUST AS WE ARE COMFORTABLE GIVING COMPLIMENTS, WE NEED TO LET OTHERS COMPLIMENT US.

I HAVE BEEN THERE, FEELING AWKWARD AS IF I WAS UNDESERVING. WE HAVE ALL BEEN THERE. CALL IT CULTURAL UPBRINGING, THINKING THAT WE NEED TO BE THE BEST, THAT THERE IS ALWAYS SOMETHING THAT NEEDS TO IMPROVE, SOME REASON WE ARE UNWORTHY. BUT LET'S JUST ACCEPT THE COMPLIMENTS AND KEEP THEM SAFELY IN OUR HEARTS, SO WHEN NO ONE BELIEVES IN US, WHEN THE PATH IS COMPLICATED AND LONELY, THOSE COMPLIMENTS WILL HELP US GET TO THE FINISH LINE.

"Hope is being able to see that there is light despite all the darkness"

-DESMOND TUTU

If you died now, would you have any regrets?

I WANT TO ENSURE I AM DOING EVERYTHING IN MY POWER TO LIVE A HAPPY, SUCCESSFUL LIFE. AND SUCCESS IS DIFFERENT FOR EVERYONE. BUT TO ME IT IS ABOUT BEING HEALTHY, ABOUT BEING SURROUNDED BY FAMILY AND FRIENDS, AND ABOUT DREAMING BIG AND WORKING DAILY ON MAKING THOSE DREAMS A REALITY. OH, AND COFFEE AND TRAVELING! LOADS OF TRAVEL. WHAT IS IT FOR YOU?

ABOUT THE AUTHOR

Carolina Veira is an authentic leader, financial strategist, and Diversity and Inclusion champion, with a passion for the advancement and empowerment of Hispanics, women, and other groups. Carolina is an award-winning professional and entrepreneur with a successful trajectory in creating community initiatives and strategic partnerships.

Carolina is the leader of The Hispanic Star Miami hub, steering the strategy, fundraising & development efforts of various initiatives benefiting the Hispanic Community. Carolina also serves as a Board Director of Deliver the Dream and the Latin American Business Association (LABA). She is also a contributing author of Hispanic Stars Rising: The New Face of Power, and Today's Inspired Latina, Volume IX. Carolina believes our voices and our stories have unlimited power and need to be shared with the world, that is why she also hosts ¡HABLEMOS! Podcast: Conversations with talented humans who are leading with heart and passion.

Carolina earned a double Bachelor of Science degree from D'Youville College in Business and Accounting and a Master's in Business Administration. She is Ecuadorian-American currently residing in Miami. She enjoys tennis, the Buffalo Bills, and speaks three languages.

www.ingramcontent.com/pod-product-compliance
Lightning Source LLC
Chambersburg PA
CBHW041235240426
43673CB00011B/346